GRIDIRON GRAMMAR

SOUTHERN STYLE

GRIDIRON GRAMMAR

SOUTHERN STYLE

A handbook to understanding coaches, players, officials, Monday-morning quarterbacks and football widows in the South!

CHARLES NICHOLSON

August House Publishers, Inc.

LITTLE ROCK

Published by August House, Inc.,
P.O. Box 3223, Little Rock, Arkansas, 72203,
501-372-5450.

Printed in the United States of America

10 9 8 7 6 5 4 3 2 1

LIBRARY OF CONGRESS CATALOGING-IN-PUBLICATION DATA

Nicholson, Charles, 1946-
Gridiron grammar, Southern style / by Charles Nicholson. — 1st ed.
p.   cm.
"Use this handbook to understand coaches, players, officials,
Monday morning quarterbacks, and football widows in the South!"
ISBN 0-87483-158-X (alk. paper) : $9.95
1. Football—Southern States—Terminology. 2. Football players—
Southern States—Language (New words, slang, etc.) 3. Football—
Southern States—Humor. I. Title.
GV959.N45 1990
796.332'0975—dc20   90-36279

First Edition, 1990

Executive: Ted Parkhurst
Project editor: Judith Faust
Cover design and text drawings: Wendell E. Hall
Typography: Lettergraphics, Little Rock

Characters portrayed in this book are fictional.
Any resemblance to actual persons, living or dead,
is entirely coincidental and a crying shame.

This book is printed on archival-quality paper which meets the
guidelines for performance and durability of the Committee on
Production Guidelines for Book Longevity of the
Council on Library Resources.

AUGUST HOUSE, INC.   PUBLISHERS   LITTLE ROCK

For Jack Scratch and Phil Thelucre

Mission Improbable

The envelope came postage due, no return address. The smeared postmark held no clue, but the plain white label could only have been typed by a large, left-handed man with a spelling disorder and black moustaches.

"Mr. Charles Nicholson, Exchoir," it read, "Or Current Resonant."

I took the mysterious envelope to my reading room and opened it. The contents were puzzling: eight-by-ten glossy of Robert E. Lee, twenty-seven bus tickets, unmarked video tape, forged press pass, nose and glasses. I placed everything but the video back in the envelope, flushed, then retired to the den.

I played the tape. As I had suspected, a large man with black moustaches was speaking, his voice like concrete galoshes. "Your mission," he said, "should you decide to accept it, is to use the contents of this envelope to study the sport of football as it exists in the South today, and to publish a definitive report that will alleviate the current rash of regional linguistic peccadillos and teach them Yankees how to talk."

The tape self-destructed when I pushed the rewind button, setting fire to my VCR and ruining the kudzu my wife was rooting in a jar on the TV set. But my duty was clear, and the report that follows is the improbable result of that mission.

Enjoy,

Charles Nicholson, Exchoir

Contents

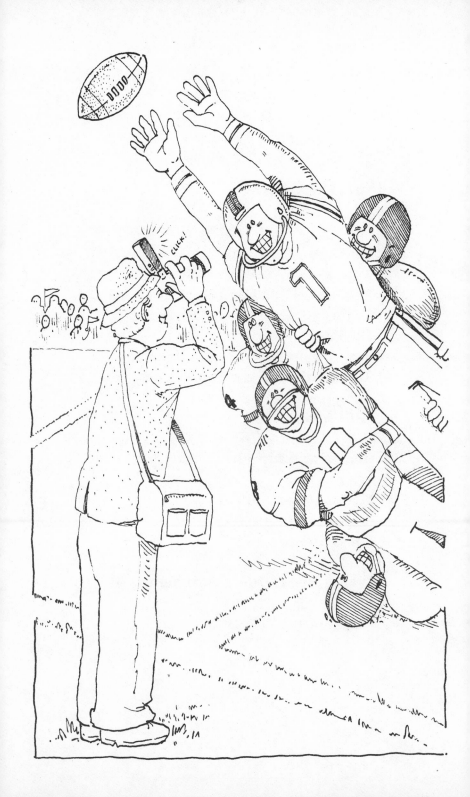

Chapter One

In the South, football doesn't take priority, it gets it as a gift. So when the Grim Reaper came to call on our old friend Sherwin Pointspredder IV during the second half of the Super Bowl, it didn't surprise Death himself when Sherwin clutched his chest and screamed, "Holdawnaminnitwillya? DonchanoIgottwennybuxaridinawn...

THE GAME?

britches: holes. "Britches in our lan, hell. They was a three-piece suit."

carry: to transport a human being via automobile. "Junior Jr. carried Nadine to the bawlgame in his pickemup truck so's she could watch him tote the bawl."

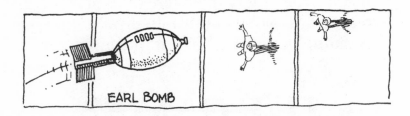

EARL BOMB

earl bomb: **1.** big firecracker. **2.** long, high pass. "Bubba leans so fur back when he thows them earl bombs, he's got turf toes on his knuckles."

eckstablish: to earn respect in an area of expertise. "Soon's we eckstablish the run, we'll try a ford payus."

farce in tan: the situation a team faces at
the beginning of every series of downs.

> Farce in tan,
> Do what you can.
> Secont in lawng,
> Don't go wrawng.
> Thard in ainches,
> Stay in the trainches.
> But foeth in a mile,
> Jus' kick it in smile!

far pyre: the ability to throw a football long
and hard. "Our new quawtuhback has tremen-
dous far pyre, but he's about as ackrat as a lawng
range weather foecast."

foamation: the arrangement of players on
the field. "Bubba said they went to the wishbone
awfense awnacounna he cain't see good outta the
eye foamation."

ford payus: when the ball is thrown beyond the line of scrimmage. "You can ladearl as minny tams as you want to, Elrod, but you can only make a ford payus oncet."

go fart: pour on the gas at a critical moment. "It was foeth down and ainches. An eerie silence fell over the crowd as they waited for the team to go fart."

go lan: the stripe at each end of the field, which a team must cross with the football to score. "Them folks over in the Middle East must show take thar footbawl serious, Elrod, the way thay're always fattin' over them Go Lan Hats."

ladearl: a sideward toss of the football. "The mainliest difference atween a ladearl and a ford payus is that a ladearl cain't go pass the lan of skirmish."

14

lanna nup: getting ready to play football. "They was lanna nup with twelve men on the field, Elrod. That's why Bubba was trine to go to his her-yup awfense."

lawng thow: lengthy ford payus. "Man, that was a lawng thow ol' Bubba made lass nat. Went eighty-sumpin yards afore it was pick tawf."

mint: sixty seconts. "If they'd start giving the two mint wawnin earlier in the game, it wouldn't always put us in such a rush."

momentum: the impetus which allows one team to pull farther and farther ahead of another. "*Mo*mentum, hell. If we had any *less* mentum we'd have to speed up to stop."

offensive lines: **1.** "You're so ugly you look lack your body just rejected a face transplant." **2.** "Wanna buy some nekkid pitchers of your wife?" **3.** etc.

pick tawf: intercepted. "That's the third payus they've pick tawf taday."

plain feel: where the game takes place. "Thar new stadium was nice, but the plain feel was so bad the team had to play in hipboots and pass out green glasses to the fans."

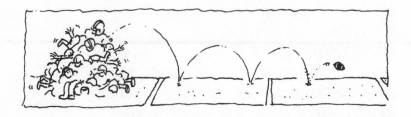

point air: what you try to get air you get a touchdown.

sackerfast: when something of value was given up for something of a potentially lesser value. "Dyne by the blitz means we just sackerfast coverage for a fast sack and blowed it."

sar grapes: belittling an elusive goal. "Sar grapes, Elrod, is lack when we lost to the deaf and blind school cause they was stealing our signals."

scorn: something which expresses a team's superiority. "Bob Earl says he can deal with the other team's scorn, as lawng as they don't spack the bawl or daince in the end zone air they do it."

shoat: **1.** little bitty pig. **2.** little bitty bit. "Them Warthawgs must rung Bubba's bell on that last play. Elst why would he thow a earl bomb when we was a inch shoat a the go lan?"

spy sewn farce: secretive attempt to fool the defense. "Thay're lanna nup to defend the run, so let spy sewn farce and run on secont."

swang: rapid, often unexpected change. "We ain't had the momentum swang away from us this fast since Bubba was splashing toilet water on his face at half time and the lid fell on his throne hand."

throne: propelling the ball with one's arm and hand. "The way Bubba's throne tonat, we'd be better awf a stain awn the groun."

titan: a close ballgame. "I wouldn't say it was a good offensive football game or a good defensive game either, but four to two is a titan, awlrat."

yard rushin: **1.** short ground gain. **2.** bolshevik groundskeeper.

yoont: a special group of players. "Her yup. We only got three seconts to get the feel go yount awnna feel."

Chapter Two

Southern football expert and syndicated talk show host Leotis Roundsound once said the best way for anyone to really get to know the South was to study the traditions behind her great football

TEAMS and BOWL GAMES

(Of course, Leotis also once said the main difference between Yankeeland and Hell was the weather, but was forced to retract his statement and apologize to the Devil.)

Aggies: **1.** Texas A&M. **2.** prized game piece. "Don't be so ignernt, Elrod. He said the Aggies was plain for all the marbles, not they was plain marbles for all the Aggies."

Arn Bo: big intrastate rivalry between Auburn University and the University of Alabama, usually played in Birmingham, where they make a lot of arn and steel.

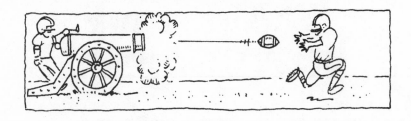

Arnge Bo: bowl game played in My Yammy, down in Flardy, where the Arnges and the Alley Gaders grow.

Big Arnge: the University of Tennesee, whose proud colors are arnge and white. "Not arns, Elrod, arnges. Thay're throne arnges at us."

Big Ten: group of eleven Yankee football schools.

Cavaliers: the University of Virginia, noted for their attitude.

Commadoughs: Vanderbilt University, perennial Southeastern Conference underdog which has nevertheless pulled its share of upsets. "Be careful betting agin them Commadoughs, Elrod. On any given Saddidy they'll take thar stand."

Cotton Bo: held in Dallas ever since the bo weevul came.

Cowbose: Dallas professional team. "Junior Jr. said he always did wanna play for the Cowbose, but he'd settle for the Orlers or Saince if he could stay in the South."

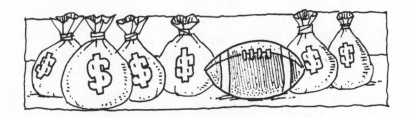

Crimson Tad: the University of Alabama, always a contender. "Yawl can bet the farm on the Crimson Tad, Elrod. They'll warsh over that bunch of Yankees lack a cow rocking on a flat pea."

Dawgs: the University of Georgia, or Mississippi State. "Bothobm's half bull and half dawg, and about as hard to keep down as week-old collards."

Fatten Taggers: Louisiana State University, the only team in the Southeastern Conference with an automatic two-touchdown home field advantage. "Loud? Hell, I was talking to myself and couldn't figure out what I was trine to say till I looked in a mirror and read my lips."

Gader Bo: bowl game played in Jacksonville, where the Alley Gaders grow Arnge and Blue.

Green Wave: Tulane University, recipient of the Southland's first federal roadbuilding grant, which was subsequently used to build the South's first Tulane Highway.

Hurcunce: the University of Miami. "No, Elrod, My Yammy ain't in Ohire. I blieve it's in Noo Yoke."

25

Killer Ducks: football team from
Oregon, which is about as far from the South as
you can get without changing busses, but
anybody with a team named Killer Ducks has
got to be a bunch of Good Ol' Boys.

Lawng Hones: the University of Texas.
"It's a kind of cow, Elrod, lack them Brammerses
and Black Agnesses."

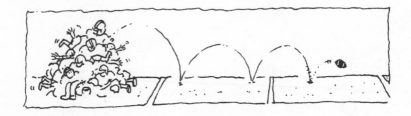

My Yammy Dawfins: pro team
headquartered in the Yankee suburb of
My Yammy.

NCAA: where you go when you have a
drinking problem in Raleigh.

number one: digit indicating apparent IQ of fans who pay good money for oversized foam rubber hands suited only for picking the Green Giant's nose.

Nyawlin Saince: team that plays pro football in the Supah Dome, where they play the Shugah Bo and sometimes the Supah Bo, too.

Peach Bo: played in Atlanta, home of the famous Joyjuh peach.

Razorbacks: the University of Arkansas. "They spell it with a 'ess' on the end, but they mean 'double-you,' Elrod, and Razorback is a kind of a hawg, not what a teed-awf kitty cat does."

Rebels: the University of Mississippi, and there ain't but one way to say Rebels, suh: Loud!

Shugah Bo: post-season extravaganza hosted annually in New Orleans by the Champion of the Southeastern Conference. Named for all the sweet thangs and shugahs down on Bourbon Street.

Simmernose: Florida State University. "The Simmernose was a Injun tribe, Elrod, lack the Etlanna Braifs."

Supah Bo: Where the best team in the NFC plays the best team in the AFC in the dullest game you ever did see.

Taggers: Auburn University, and also Clemson. To confuse Yankee announcers, Auburn adopted an eagle as its mascot. "We now switch you live to the sidelines where, while Auburn goes for two and a one-point win in the last three seconds of the ball game, our man for the forty-seventh time this season asks the guy with the eagle on his arm to explain...hu-oh. Hold on a minute folks. Don't adjust your sets. We ought to be able to show you that last play right after these messages."

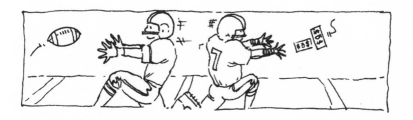

Wald Cats: the University of Kentucky, in a border state. "I hates to be the one to tell you this, Elrod, but most awl them Kentucky kernels fought for the Nawth."

Chapter Three

There is a large group of Southerners whose idea of fun is driving two hundred miles through torrential rains to pay for the privilege of sitting on hard seats, eating cold food and screaming themselves hoarse for a team that hasn't had a winning season in twelve years. They're known affectionately as...

THE FANS

aiminna: planning on doing something but probably not right now or even next week unless somebody makes you. "Them bookies ain't nothing but a bunch of loan sharks, Elrod. When I toll 'em I was aiminna pay 'em Saddidy they beat my haid so far down I hadda unzip my britches to blow my nose."

bag ladies: sad commentary on man's inhumanity to man that is witnessed all too frequently by persons attending football games in large Southern cities. "Look at all them bag ladies. How on earth can they see the game through them two little holes?"

been dixie-un: what devout fans once did before a game. "Yawl bow yawl's haids now, whilst Brother Bubba Billybob Cracker says the been dixie-un."

bleachers: **1.** outdoor pews. **2.** blondheaded cheerleaders. "Dagburnit, Elrod. When you said we ought to find us some bleachers to climb on, I thought you meant the kind wears painties and socks."

canoe: **1.** question of ability. **2.** Indian boat. "Our last head cheerleader was so agyle she could open a beer can whilst dune a han stan an not miss a beat when a man ran, even if the ban played a can can. Canoe?"

depot: people who don't have a much money as derich.

ethylene glycol: Bronx cheerleader who resigned and moved South to protest the skimpy outfits she was forced to wear during cold northern winters. Claims to be antifreeze.

ferner: rarely seen at football games in Dixie. Term indicates: **1.** someone who was born outside the South, or **2.** one who ferns.

football widows: used to describe people who neither enjoy nor understand the game. "It ain't no use trine to talk footbawl widows wives a ours."

haint: **1.** past tense of ain't. **2.** past tense of dead.

holler: **1.** empty inside. **2.** yell real loud. "It's awlrat ta cheer, but you don't have to holler your brains out."

hot and chili: how dawgs come or weather is. "The foecast says it'll be chili for the pep rally tonat, but you can bet it'll be hot tamale."

hynus: neither frontus nor sadus. "Yonder comes a usher, Elrod. Tell him we hadda move down here awnacounna there was a bunch of drunks hynus."

juggernaut: something which exacts a great sacrifice. "Since they made that stoopa drool bout not taking likker into the stadium, I don't know if it's worth the trouble to bring a juggernaut."

mascots: silly-looking animals with people dressed up like them inside. "I'm sorry you cain't breathe, Elrod, but you know what Harry Truman always said: 'If you cain't stand the beak, stay out of the chicken.'"

menu: bofus.

my lenore: **1.** Edgar Allan Poe's dead girlfriend. **2.** a measure of speed. "We drove nearabout thutty my lenore on the innerstate and still missed the kickawf."

nachos: somebody else's.

prare: illegal request for divine intervention. "I don't care what the Supremes say, Elrod. When you behind ninety-three points in the first quawtuh, it's tam to bow you haid in prare."

precursors: football fans who are not yet old enough to curse. In some areas of the South, these are also know as "lap babies."

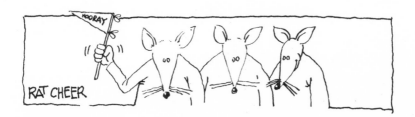

rat cheer: not over yonder or even over thar. "Yawl can leave that beer cooler rat cheer, boys. Mean Elrod'll take care of it whilst yawl're watching the game."

rites of fall: emotionally charged events often observed on college campuses during football season, especially during homecoming. "Ol' Dean Dryfuss said he's coming by our party after the game, and if it looks lack we're having another drunken brawl, he's gonna call the rite poeleases."

samoa: **1.** tropical island. **2.** extra amount. "They gonna ship us to the South Pacific if we don't scoe samoa points."

sitar: what you do at a football game when you gitar.

sporter: **1.** fan. **2.** jockey strap. "It ain't a slingshot or a nose guard either, Elrod. It's a alfledic sporter."

sport snooze: the way serious football fans keep up with the world of sport. "The reason they always put the sport snooze on last is they know nobody ainnagonna go to sleep until it's over."

stern committee: group of forward thinking people within a larger group, whose mission it is to think up ways to move the whole group forward. "Check the bylaws, Elrod. See can they thow me awf the stern committee just for suggestin' that nekkid cheerleaders would liven up our tailgape parties."

stoopa digits: the other team's fans. "I'm glad we got more class than to put fanger paint all over our faces lack them stoopa digits. These goriller suits is enough."

taint: conjunction of *it* and *am not*. "Taint haints I'm worried about, Elrod. It's just bad luck not to whittle past a graveyard."

Chapter Four

These days it seems that before football season is even over, two things are alrady on everybody's mind...

RECRUITING and THE DRAFT

Now the draft is pretty cut and dried, but ol' Elrod A. Reddennekker just might have a point when he says there wouldn't even have to be any recruiting if people would be more careful and cruit right the first time.

academic: what education seems to have become in many college football programs.

bidet: small bid. Rhymes with toilet.

big bucks: dictionaries, encyclopedias, stuff like that.

bofubm: allubm when there is just twoubm.

contrack: a legally binding agreement in which attorneys of the party of the first part (the team) attempt to enslave the party of the second part (the player or coach) for the duration of his career, whereinas the attorneys for the party of the second part go to such great lengths to impoverish the party of the first part that after working toward an agreement for six months the attorneys for the parties of both parts are usually the only ones who end up making any money off the deal.

faults: something done wrong. "Coach said not to give them recruits any faults impresssions, so don't lie lest they axe something inbarsin."

from can to cain't: as long as you possibly can till you cain't no more. "Ever coach we got has been on the road from can to cain't, but ain't but two new players signed and one of them thought he was buying life insurance."

furl: mean, nasty, and wild. "Them pro scouts is looking for somebody that don't unfurl when the game plan does."

lieberry: large, book-filled buildings that are sometimes inadvertently included in a recruit's campus tour. "The difference between a lieberry and a dinkleberry, Elrod, is that one is a bad place to get stuck in and the other gets stuck in a bad place."

lumnah: anyone who ever went to a school, even if it was only to use the bathroom or deliver a pizza. "Coach says it was a mistake to let the lumnah get involved in our recruiting. Ain't no high school kid needs to see what he's gonna look lack when he gets old."

moan lackly: probably probable. "That boy's daddy played for Holler Oak, Elrod, so it's moan lackly he will too. The tree don't fall fur from the acorn, you know."

Murcan: citizen of the United States. "Junior Jr. said if he makes Awl Murcan agin this year, it'll be a bonafide murcle."

nebmine: forget. "Nebmine how quick that boy can run a hunnert yards, he cain't hold onto a footbawl but for twoubm."

pawn mall: anticipated parental influence. "He told us rat awf his pawn mall be the ones decide which school he gets to play for."

pickaninny: archaic, offensive term rarely used in the South today except to chastise a professional football team for wasting a valuable draft choice on a stoopa digit.

reckon his chances: used to discuss any potentially self-destructive action by a prospect. "Reckon do that boy know that sassin' Coach is reckon his chances to ever play for us?"

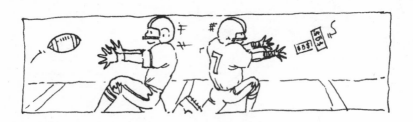

sposta: should but might not. "We sposta sign three hot prospecks taday, Elrod, and the spense is killin' me."

strack: **1.** hit somebody. **2.** refuse to hit anybody. "Bubba's got hisself such a good contrack he gets paid whilst the team's on strack even if he don't call the first hack."

yung fu: adolescent ignoramus. Not to be confused with "hung fu," which is what laxatives are for.

Chapter Five

When they asked star college linebacker Bob Earl Brutstrinth to name the necessities of life he replied, "Sex and violence," without hesitation.

"But what about food, shelter, and clothing?" the effete and somewhat naive denizen of Ivory Towertown inquired. "Surely one has to worry about them."

"Nah, Prof," Bob Earl said with a laugh. "I get them free with my football scholarship, just like the rest of...

THE PLAYERS

allamoney: what many professional football players think they have, only to learn to their dismay that it's really just the correct pronunciation of "alimony."

ambrosia: the food of Greek and Roman gods. Now a term used by Southern football players to indicate a harmonious relationship among team members. "It's lack we all ambrosia."

are row sea: type of cocola. Often a problem for freshmen players during registration when—hot and thirsty from trying to find the easiest basketweaving teacher—they line up for a refreshing soft drink, only to find they have inadvertently committed themselves to four years of Are Row Tea Sea and two years of active duty.

badmitten: excuse given by Elmer "White Gloves" Borden for dropping seventy-three consecutive passes, twelve laterals, and an undisclosed number of names.

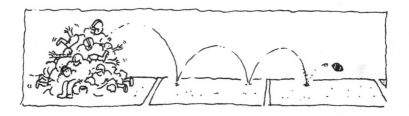

dade ranger: depending upon the use of the hard or soft *g* in its pronunciation, this term can refer to either a deceased cowboy or a person who looks exactly like someone else. "Bubba's a dade ranger for that guy who always wore a black mast and shot silver pullets, ain't he?"

Dafrilla Vickry: estranged wife of professional tackling dummy and ex-champion ski jumper, I. Gunny DePhietz.

decalfalong: a grueling test of athletic ability. "Bob Earl done alright on the shot put and discuss parts, but he messed up on the lawng jump when he tried to brang decalfalong."

flanders: men who play the field. "Maybelle said if she'd a knowed what a flander Bubba was, she'd a marred that rich flanthrowpiss she was goin with."

goriller: **1.** huge, simian football player. **2.** first words to an old love song. "If Bob Earl's the goriller anybody's dream, it'd have to be a nat mar."

hot snot: what some players think they are even after they ain't "He used to be pretty hot, but now he snot."

how fast: a measure of a player's determination and skill. "Now that was a how fast try if I ever saw one."

ladder man: varsity athlete. "That boy was so ignernt he thought a foe ladder man was a alfleke who could say the alphabet without missing but foe ladders."

longshoremen: tall players with self confidence.

moe foe: abusive epithet often exchanged during heated arguments between opposing players. Origin of the term is unclear, but it seems to date back at least to the forties and may have been intended as a slur on those crass individuals so insensitive as to dislike the Three Stooges.

painty waist: sissy. "Bob Earl cain't stand sissies, but I toll him a painty waist was a turbul thang to mind."

parallel Bars: two small football players from Chicago.

pier steers: what some players get to show off their wealth. "I guess he can afford diamonds and gold, but Bubba with pier steers is about lack a goriller wearing lipstick: he looks redickless and he damn sure better not try to kiss me."

quawtuhback: **1.** important offensive football player. **2.** what you are lucky to get from a dollar when you buy a stick of gum at the concession stand. "The reason Bubba is playing quawtuhback instead of haffback or fullback is awnacounna he's the only one on the team who can count to hike."

retar:　**1.** quit football forever. **2.** buy new rubber. **3.** both.

santy clause:　part of some player's contracts. "After Bob Earl come back from having his last lobotomy, the owners put a santy clause in his contrack."

spear chunker:　opposite of infear chunker.

stick up:　method of measuring a player's speed. "That tackle is so slow you have to put a stick up beside him to see is he moving."

tat:　not loose. "Bob Earl grabbed that tat end and shook him everwhichaway but loose."

turbul sinner: bad football player. "That Elrod Jr. is a turbul sinner. Ever tam he snaps the bawl, he either thows it through the quawtuh-back's laigs or hits hisself in the dololly."

ward ego: problem with a few prima donna types who feel free to do just as they please. "I toll Bubba to wait rat cheer by the go postes. Now ward ego?"

water boys: sexist question. You couldn't get away with asking water girls, could you?

woof: **1.** wild dog. **2.** method of eating. "The way them boys eats at the training table, if you let your hand tarry over the biscuits one obms libel to woof down your fanger."

yo momma: implied insult. Most effective when shouted across the line of scrimmage in reply to opponent's previous major insult.
>   "Sum bitch."
>   "Yo momma."

yo momma nem: implied concern. "Hows yo momma nem been dune?"

Chapter Six

HEALTH and INJURIES

are of the utmost importance to any player's career, for as outstanding halfback Junior Farnwyde, Jr., is fond of pointing out, "Ain't hardly nobody ever gives you the bawl when your laig's broke."

assburn: what you take for a headache.

ass in a sling: what a quarterback can get when he goes mano a mano with a defensive tackle twice his size. "Tell the trainer to put some ass in that sling, Bubba, to help keep the swelling down."

bare minimum: common during a player's physical exam. "It wasn't bad till we got down to the bare minimum, Elrod, but swallering that purple stuff was about as much fun as poison idey in a noodess camp."

caterac: serious eye problem. "When Doc ast Coach if he'd ever had a caterac removed, he said no, but somebody stold his new Mercedes when he wasn't looking oncet."

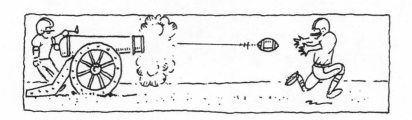

code: common viral infection. "Codes is caused by a rhinovarserus, Elrod. Lack the one downt the zoo only littler."

condominiums: birth control for pygmies.

dierear: one of the worst things a player can get during a game. "Bob Earl ate thutty-foe chili tamales and got dierear so bad he blowed the back off the outhouse and wilted all the flowers in the seed catalog."

61

discussion: what you get when some-body hits you in the head with a discus.

dune asbestos: in top form even though it probably doesn't seem like it. "Quit crittersizing me, Elrod. Cain't you see I'm dune asbestos I can?"

eat up with the dummass:
possessing negative intelligence. "That Bob Earl's eat up with the dummass. Flunked his urine test cause he took a pill to keep him awake studying for it."

fall in champagne: what a kicker does every time a defensive player gets within ten yards of him.

gonad: sexual term. "We gonad salt peter to the mash taters so them boys'll quit fooling around on game nats."

groan injury: result of a helmet to the dololly.

hemorrhoid surfers: people who spend a disproportionate amount of time in warm water and never laugh at silver bullet commercials.

hernear: what you'd better not try to hold if you got one and ain't wearing a truss.

hocker:　a big spit. "Don't let the cammer see that hocker, Elrod. Put it in your pocket."

kudzu:　ivy on steroids.

let stress out:　seek relief from tension. "We need to relax. Let stress out in our sweats and run a few laps."

logarithm:　term used in multiplication. "Bubba says him and Maybelle didn't intend to have any chillwrens till he got to the pros, but they couldn't afford a condominium when they first got married and the logarithm method didn't work out."

lungar: big green spit. See "hocker" and "code."

oaker: healthful green vegetable. "That oaker mat be good for you, but it drools worse than a teething baby."

pianissimo: what the doctor says to a player who is undergoing his second drug test of the day.

Ralph, Huey, and Harvey: the three names most frequently called when a Southerner blows hash (aka "vomicks").

Soho District: area where overworked prostitutes live.

sore asses: chronic, often painful skin condition. "Coach is scratching cause he's surfin from the heartbreak of sore asses."

strange paradox: two weird physicians.

summer sore: where bluebirds fly, or any other indefinite location. "I blieve I left the calamine lotion summer sore yonder."

turf toe: painful injury often sustained when a player stumbles where the artificial turf is ripped or toe.

Chapter Seven

THE COACHES

It's a tough job. The last time they hired a Yankee to coach a Southern football team he had to start buying his clothes two sizes smaller before the first season was out. Said he hadn't really lost any weight; just found out he wasn't as big a man down here as he was up North.

Afar Asea: one who jumps ship. "When that bunch of Yankees hard our last coach away from us he took his whole staff with him. He warn't nothing but Afar Asea among the Phillip Steins."

alfledic director: the head coach's boss.

barn down: trying harder than you've been trying when you've already been trying real hard. "Coach toll the lumnah if he can get the team to really start barn down we can probably scoe a touchdown this year."

beholden: an illegal act not always frowned on by the coaching staff. "Don't yawl beholden unless it looks lack they gonna sack the quawtuhback agin."

bidness offus: the place where pay-checks come from and coaches go to get fard.

blow gum: pink chewy stuff you can make bubbles with if you don't blow it. "Coach said if it wasn't for sex and blow gum now he wouldn't get any exercise atall."

EARL BOMB

buy nout: something that happens in the middle that is the end. "Coach says ther's some tawk about buy nout his contrack just cause we've lost our last eighty-seven bawl games."

dunlapt: a condition associated with over-indulgence and a lack of exercise. "It ain't been but a year since ol' Billy Boy quit plain to coach, and already his belly dunlapt over his belt."

fig a rout: the most important thing a coach has to do once the game begins. "Coach says we could stop this rout if we could fig a rout how thay're figger nout our passing routes."

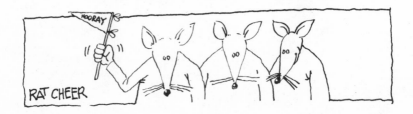

RAT CHEER

fork tine: comment uttered by Coach Beauregard "Kiss Your Sister" Jackson before ordering his team to go for two with six seconds remaining in the game. Unfortunately, they lost by forty-seven.

game fems: what most coaches like to spend time with after a big game. "Put your natty back awn, Sweetpaints. I cain't come to bed till after I study these game fems."

harden fard: the entire ordeal of being graciously recruited, gainfully employed, and summarily dismissed. "Coach has been harden fard so many tams they named one of the tiles on the space shuttle after him."

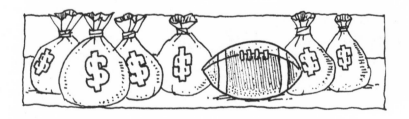

hepper: one who heps. "Coach don't seem to fall down on the sadlans near as much now he's got that hepper to keep his headphone wars untangled."

hire education: theory which seeks to explain why the salary of a head coach is five times that of the university's president.

hot style: what most coaches look for in a player. "Coach says he don't much care how big a man is, long as he's hot style, a-gyle, and mo-byle."

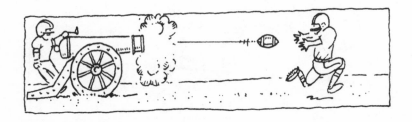

implode: opposite of explode. "Coach implode the backup quawtuhback not to quit the team until he's explode his other possibilities."

in arrears: common problem for offensive coordinators. "Coach, we cain't hyar Bubba's awedoubles with awl that crowd noise in arrears."

intears: opposite of extears. "Coach is crine cause when he toll the alfledic drecktor we needed to get more work out of the intear linemen, the ignoramus put new telephones in the locker room."

pearl: extreme danger. "Coach said so many thangs went wrong this game it reminded him of that old song, 'Strang a Pearls.'"

rainforce: strengthen. "Coach says our defensive lan is so weak we couldn't rainforce it with a concreke wall."

seed: what a good coach can inspire a player to do. "Coach toll that new quawtuhback if he didn't hurry up and seed our expectations, he was gonna put velcro on him and let Bob Earl use him for a laig weight."

tam: a measure of eternity. Can be long or short, depending on the circumstances and one's perspective. "Coach said he spent three whole days in Noo Yoke Ciddy one tam and never did for the Y.M.C.A. or a free toilet."

turbul: coaching term for a player, team, or situation that exhibits badness so far beyond awful that even the superlative "awflest" becomes inadequate.

war nail: a philosophical and often rhetorical question of location. "Coach axed Bob Earl war nail he was at bed check last nat, and Bob Earl axed rat back wot nail bidness was it of his."

Chapter Eight

THE OFFICIALS

Officiating football games is a lot like cleaning out septic tanks: Somebody's got to do it, but it's hard for most people to see what they get out of it.

asphalt: something that is the fault of an ass.

awf sads: opposite of awn sads.

comminst: began. "They shoulda thowed a flag the mint Bob Earl comminst pulling that quawtuhback's laig off."

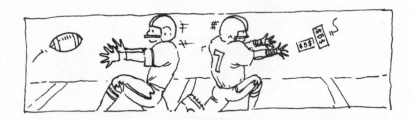

confurnce: **1.** group of teams joined together in the name of a good game. **2.** group of officials joined together in the pall of a bad call.

doodley squat: something a whole lot of people who don't know it themselves think a whole lot of officials don't know, too. See "ignernt" and "ass vs. hole in the ground."

fly gone: indicative of a penalty. "Don't spack the bawl yet, Bubba. They's a fly gone the play."

ignernt: what a person does not have to be to want to be a football official but might as well be, and blind too, because no matter how hard he tries, both sides will accuse him of being both.

in air: what officials never are. "That umpar said the onliest tam he was ever in air was when he thought he made a mistake oncet."

lar: person unknown for acute veracity. "That official said Bob Earl grabbed that boy's face mast, but he's a lar. Allst Bob Earl grabbed was his lips."

lawn odor: what comes from the officials down on the field. "I'm gonna keep lawn odor in this game if I have to penalize the cheerleaders, the mascot, and the lady that sang in the half-time show."

line judge: official whose calls are sometimes out of bounds. "We made a touchdown year afore last, Elrod, but some line judge told a whopper and called it back."

marred: subject to the devastations of matrimony. "I blieve all officials is marred, Elrod. Ain't no happy man would take that job."

poeleases: more than one law enforcement officer. "Take that awf your haid and sit down, Elrod, afore that umpar calls the poeleases."

pylon: to tackle people who are already on the ground. "Yawl watch that Bob Earl Brutstrinth. He's bad to pylon air the whistle's blowed."

ruffin the punner: **1.** running into the kicker. **2.** beating up on the smart aleck at the comedy club.

umpar: the head official.

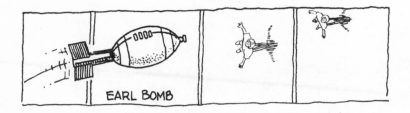

EARL BOMB

whirl: a question often affecting the outcome of a game. "Looks lack Bubba done tackled hisself agin. Reckon whirl they spot the bawl?"

wussess: plural of wuss. "That line judge made three of the two wussess calls I ever saw."

zeebers: **1.** convict horses. **2.** men who wear striped shirts and run around waving their arms a lot.

Chapter Nine

LOCKER ROOMS and EQUIPMENT

They smell like what's most often spilled on them: blood, sweat, tears, and cheap aftershave lotion, but the players love it. As star quarterback Leroy "Bubba" Deepthret told one complaining reporter, "Stink, hell. It smells just lack a stack of hunnert dollar bills ta me, lady."

bar spot: a worn place on the football field.

bawls: **1.** cries. **2.** dances. **3.** round pointy things with shoelaces. **4.** dolollies. "Beulah started bawling when Bob Earl broke their date to the Harvest Bawl, but when he said he'd give her the game bawl she quit bawling about all the bawls they'd missed and kicked him in 'em."

borry: opposite of lend. "Can I borry one of your sweatsocks, Elrod? My left one keeps falling down awnacounna it ain't got no ecstatic in it."

defense: inanimate object with the uncanny ability to stay in one place while running all the way around defield.

depose: what you have to kick the bawl through to get a feel go.

face mast: helmet handles.

hahjeans: sanitary practices. "Coach says if we don't keep this locker room cleaner, he's gonna make ever one of us take Personal Hahjeans till we pass it."

hawg bladder: the original pigskin. "We was so poor that whenever we butchered a hawg we used the bladder for a football and saved as many oinks as we could for the halftime show."

hifi: aerial handshake.

meers: reflective glass located at various places in and around the locker room. "Bubba stared in the meer so long he hypnertized hisself and fell into the glass. Says he's been surfin from sever conclusions ever since."

nat lats: illumination for games played after dark. "I cain't hardly see the game with them brat nat lats rat in my eyes."

pyre more: officially replaced the push more in 1959. Today most grass on football fields is cut with a raddin more instead of the old wawk-behine mores.

runnin shoe: what you have to do to chase flies away.

scoe bode: the large sign used to display a football game's vital statistics incorrectly. "Not only did they penalize Bob Earl thutty yards for tackling the scoe bode, they wouldn't let him play no more till he got it put back up."

spacks: pointy things on the bottom of football shoes. "A cleak is the same thang as a spack unless you do it in the end zone, Elrod."

tanny hars: the small, threadlike leavings of unclad athletes. "I don't care if they is from somebody's moustache, I ainnagonna drank outta no water fountain with lil tanny hars floating in it."

toll: past tense of tell. "They toll me this visitors' locker room was gonna be small, but I didn't know we'd have to stand sideways to smile."

woe out: used beyond redemption or repair. "We gonna have to get us a new crine towel, Coach. Thissun's plum woe out."

yournull: the thing on the locker room wall where most of the tanny hars get.

Chapter Ten

It is said with at least a modicum of truth that, in life as well as in most other endeavors, "those who can, do, while those who can't, teach." But only in America are those who can neither do nor teach raised to a position of great public responsibility and called...

THE MEDIA

awe love us: me and you and just about everybody else in the world but them.

axe: **1.** things that are split apart, usually to the detriment of the team. **2.** pose a question. "Axe them when they're gonna get their axe together, Leotis."

canasta: a game reporters often play. "I don't know if Beulah's gonna take Bob Earl back or not, but if you've got the nerve you canasta."

clubhouse dough: the only reliable way for a reporter to gain entry into the inner sanctums of locker rooms and coaches' offices. "When Coach caught me sneaking in the locker room window, he toll me if I wanted to stay I'd have to go back out and come in through the clubhouse dough."

common taters: media types whose opinions do not necessarily reflect those of anyone who actually watched the game. Often mistaken for arsh taters and common sadists.

dololly: something you either do not know or prefer not to use the proper name for. "Look that up, Leotis. We cain't go on the air and say the quawtuhback just broke his dololly off."

The English Channel: one of the things that comes between England and France. "Must not nobody watch footbawl on TV in Europe, Elrod. Thar ain't the first sadderlite disc on the Eyefull Tire, and allst you ever see on the English Channel is swimming."

95

fourth estate: numericological designation for the working press, pronounced "foe-a-the-state." "In the first place, I second the motion that we give the third degree to every member of the fourth estate who might be a fifth columnist. At least that's what my sixth sense tells me, and I'm the seventh son of a seventh son. Or was it the eighth?"

getting their shares: what most football players like to do after a game. "Bubba says he don't mind wimmin repoaters in the locker room, but he wishes they could wait till he gets outta the share to start axing quextions."

RAT CHEER

HOORAY

grape van: vehicle of rumor and innuendo. "We cain't print it yet, but I heard through the grape van that ol' Bob Earl's gonna have a sex change operation. Said not much longer will he be man."

Harmonica: female nickname. "I don't care if harmonica is 'Mouth Organ,' we ainnagonna print it here."

honor mine: a concept of importance to many media persons. "The boss says she wants to see me in her office rat now. Wonder what's honor mine?"

in bar stem: what the media manages to do to all but the unabashed, especially the bashed. "Bob Earl said that interview in bar stem, but I toll him breaking wind on national TV wasn't what he ought to be in barst about; it's telling the common tater 'he who smelt it, dealt it.'"

jamaica: **1.** island in the West Indies. **2.** use excessive force. "I never said I didn't bolivia, but just for the record alaska how jamaica talk."

july: a question of truth, usually asked off the record.
   "July?"
   "No, but April may."

libel: a big worry for media persons, especially those who cover football. "Sue us for slander, hell. Bob Earl's libel to whup awe love us when he reads this."

perzackly: in a precise manner. "I don't care whose toes I step on, Elrod, I always use perzackly the rat word. That's why they call me the owner madder poet."

Pullet Surprise: coveted journalistic award. "Man, if this turkey flies, I ought to get a Pullet Surprise."

radial tire:　where broadcasts come from. "The reason they call it being 'on the air', Elrod, is because when the common tater talks into the macker phone, it's pumped up into the station's radial tire where the air can blow it out to the coathanger on your pickemup truck. Unnerstan?"

scribe:　what you have to do to get a scription.

sticksticks:　used frequently by the media to measure and compare individual as well as team performance. "It ain't all Junior Jr.'s fault we're losing. He's averging two and a half yards a tote according to the sticksticks."

tamar sedition:　the newspaper that comes out after taday sedition.

tap wratter: what a sports wratter wrats with unless the editor lets him use the computer, which in most cases is about as likely as the alumni buying a Learjet for the water-boy.

taste vs. ratings: one ball game where the good guys never had a chance.

tawk show: popular TV and radio shows where people who don't know what they're tawking about all try to do it at the same time.

watching MTV: what you do when you get tired of listening 'm radios and reading 'm books.

what Dick saw: nineteenth century exposé regarding the exploits of infamous Yankee spy N. Richard Doapthreet, which first posed that oft-repeated question, "What terrible things did, when he went to look away down South, N. Dick see?"

ya know?:   phrase that athletes who make millions of dollars a year utter redundantly *ad infinitum* in order to give reporters with holes in their shoes and gravy stains on their shirts something to feel superior about.

MORE HUMOR FROM
AUGUST HOUSE PUBLISHERS

A Field Guide to Southern Speech
A twenty-gauge lexicon for the duck blind, the deer stand, the skeet shoot, the bass boat, and the backyard barbecue.
ISBN 0-87483-098-2, TPB, $6.95

Laughter in Appalachia
Appalachia's special brand of humor—dry, colorful, and earthy—from Loyal Jones and Billy Edd Wheeler
ISBN 0-87483-031-1, HB, $19.95
ISBN 0-87483-032-X, TPB, $8.95

Cowboy Folk Humor
Jokes, tall tales, and anecdotes about cowboys, their pranks, their foibles, and their times.
ISBN 0-87483-104-0, TPB, $8.95

The Night of the Possum Concert
"Charles Allbright has a fine comic touch like no one else I know." —Charles Portis
"The man is funny, very funny."—Phil Thomas, Associated Press
ISBN 0-87483-028-1, TPB, $8.95

Gravely the Mules Stopped Dancing
"Allbright writes in the tradition of the Southern humorists, but he outshines them all in his ability to make his readers feel good about other people."—Dee Brown
ISBN 0-87483-063-X, HB, $19.95
ISBN 0-87483-062-1, TPB, $8.95

The Preacher Joke Book
A surprisingly reverent collection of religious humor, poking fun less at the message than at the messengers.
ISBN 0-87483-087-7, TPB, $6.95

Dog Tales
Some tall, some true, all collected from the oral tradition, these stories do justice to our beloved canine friends. Just right for reading aloud.
ISBN 0-87483-076-1, TPB, $6.95

Ozark Tall Tales
Authentic mountain stories as hill folk have told them for generations.
ISBN 0-87483-099-0, TPB, $8.95

Outhouse Humor
Jokes, stories, and songs in tribute to the "little brown shack out back."
ISBN 0-87483-058-3, TPB, $5.95

August House Publishers, P.O. Box 3223, Little Rock, Arkansas 72203
1-800-284-8784